# ABOUT THIS NO NONSENSE
# SUCCESS GUIDE

This No Nonsense Success Guide, like each Success Guide, has been designed to live up to *both* parts of its name ... to provide you with useful No Nonsense information *and* to increase your personal chances for Success!

This easy-to-use, easy-to-read book is a fast, comfortable and confidential way for you to take stock of your strengths and weaknesses as a prospective independent businessperson.

Taking THE SELF-EMPLOYMENT TEST is your first important step in the challenging and rewarding process of creating, building and securing your personal financial independence — as a self-employed entrepreneur in a world where many of today's wealthiest and happiest people are in business for themselves!

## NO NONSENSE SUCCESS GUIDES:

*The Self-Employment Test*
*Getting Into The Mail Order Business*
*How To Run A Business Out Of Your Home*
*How To Own and Operate A Franchise*
*How (and Where) To Get The Money To Get Started*
*Getting Into The Consulting Business*

# NO NONSENSE

## SUCCESS GUIDE

# THE SELF-EMPLOYMENT TEST

## The 64 Questions (and Answers) You Need Before Going Into Business For Yourself

## STEVE KAHN

**LONGMEADOW PRESS**

The Self-Employment Test

Cover design by Tom Fowler, Inc.

Composition by Tod Clonan Associates, Inc.

Published for Longmeadow Press, 201 High Ridge Road, Stamford, Connecticut 06904.

ISBN: 0-681-40124-9

Printed in the United States of America

9 8 7 6 5 4 3 2 1

# TABLE OF CONTENTS

# HOW
# TO USE
# THIS BOOK

Unlike most of the "tests" which you took as a child, this book is intended to be enjoyable and confidence-building.

Best of all, there are no absolute "right" or "wrong" answers.

This book is designed simply to give you a "feeling" for the possibility of becoming an entrepreneur — someone thinking about taking on the enormous and challenging task of going into business for himself.

(By the way, although we use "he" and "him" throughout, this is an "equal opportunity book" — designed for women thinking about going into business for themselves as well as their fathers, brothers, husbands and sons.)

The more often your responses fit into the "entrepreneurial profile," the more reasonable your future chances of success as an independent businessperson.

Our concluding chapter — The Self-Employment Test Checklist— will help you to determine whether you are ready to become one of the more than 12,500 people each week who make the decision to go into business for themselves.

The Checklist is designed to be used more than once, to serve as a continuous barometer of your entrepreneurial potential. We suggest you take the Checklist "test" *now,* before beginning the book. List your answers on a separate sheet of paper. Then, after reading the book, take the "test" again. Comparing your "before-and-after" results will provide you with a useful measure of your entrepreneurial potential.

Good luck!

QUESTION

# 1

# WHY ARE YOU
# THINKING ABOUT GOING
# INTO BUSINESS
# FOR YOURSELF?

By definition, the decision to go into business for yourself is a very positive one.

It is an expression of your own courage, of your willingness to take great risk. Obviously, your hope is that this great risk will eventually bring you great rewards — both financially and emotionally.

At the beginning of the process of going into business for yourself — and for a long time thereafter — your courage is on the line.

You may not even be feeling especially courageous — and that's a good sign, an inner expression of your determination and confidence.

Don't doubt it: At the moment of deciding to go into business for yourself, you are one of the most courageous individuals in the world of commerce and free enterprise!

Courage obviously requires strength, *your* strength.

Therefore, sorting out your reasons, your motivation, your needs for making the decision to go into business for yourself is an important part of the process.

FOR YOU TO HOPE TO MAKE YOUR OWN BUSINESS WORK AND PROSPER AND BRING YOU THE REWARDS YOU ARE LOOKING TO ACHIEVE, THE REASONS FOR THE DECISION TO GO INTO BUSINESS FOR YOURSELF HAVE TO BE POSITIVE!

You have to believe that you will be able to provide a service or product with greater skill and commitment than anyone else.

You have to believe that you have the ability to own, operate, manage and market a service or product better than anyone else.

You have to believe in yourself.

You have to believe in your ability to stick with it.

You have to believe in your family.

And you have to know — *without any significant doubts* — that you are making the decision to go into business for yourself out of confidence, out of a sense of self-destiny and out of a desire to build a better, more fulfilling life for yourself and your family.

If you don't feel this way, then perhaps the best move for you is to postpone your decision to go into business for yourself.

If you do, then the next 63 questions are going to be the most exciting and productive questions you've ever asked yourself!

# 2

# WHO DO YOU SEE
# WHEN YOU LOOK
# IN THE MIRROR?

This isn't a trick question.

Who do you *really* see when you look into the mirror?

Do you like who you see?

I hope that the answer, without hesitation, is YES!

Because if you don't like who you see, you had better stop right here before pursuing the path of business independence — and begin some real work on your own sense of self-esteem.

"Going into business for yourself" isn't an idle phrase — it's an accurate representation of what will happen when you make the decision to give up your regular paycheck and the security and comfort of your regular workplace.

There won't be anyone around to cheer you up. There won't be a friendly voice saying, "Better luck tomorrow" or "Don't take it so hard, it's not coming out of your paycheck" or "Sleep on it."

You're going to be on your own.

So you've really got to like and trust that face you see in the mirror each morning. It's going to be your best friend — sometimes your only friend — during those difficult, often discouraging early days of beginning a business.

Sure, if you have a family, they'll be on your side.

And so will your lawyer, your accountant and your banker.

Their good will — even though it is sincere and well-intentioned — is ultimately an illusion ... because they are all looking to *you* to make it happen. And the bottom line is that, in truth and in fact, you will have no one to ultimately look to other than yourself.

So, at the beginning of going into business for yourself (and very likely for the entire time that you are in business for yourself), you're going to have to be your own best friend, cheerleader and psychological provider.

It will be virtually impossible for you to succeed if you don't like who you see in the mirror.

So, look again . . . before leaping . . . and make certain that you like who you see!

QUESTION

# 3

# IS YOUR DECISION TO GO INTO BUSINESS FOR YOURSELF ONE OF ACTION — OR REACTION?

What were you thinking about on the day you first thought about going into business for yourself?

Were you mad at your boss?

Annoyed with the co-worker with whom you share a secretary?

Convinced, for the hundredth time, that you were doing much more for your company than it was ever going to do for you?

As honest feelings, each of these thoughts are valid.

As reasons for making the decision to go into business for yourself, they are guaranteed formulas for disaster!

Remember, long ago, when one of your teachers or parents reminded you that "two wrongs don't make a right?"

Obviously, at that time, they weren't thinking about the prospect of you going into business for yourself — but they might as well have . . . because if negative, reactive factors are propelling you towards making one of the most important decisions of your adult life, then while you may be on the right track, you are there for the wrong reasons. And you are going to be derailed!

A certain amount of dissatisfaction goes into the decision to go into business for yourself. Because if you were totally satisified with your present circumstances, you wouldn't be thinking about changing them.

The danger arises when a single negative event or a build-up of negative situations form your primary building block for making the decision to "get out" of your current workplace.

It's possible that all you really require is a different job or simply a change of assignment within your organization. Not everyone is ready, willing or — most importantly — able to go into business for himself.

So you have to guard against the danger that your decision is one of reaction rather than action independent of a "bad day" on the job or at the office.

As we've already said, the decision to go into business for yourself is a positive act. Therefore, if it is based on a negative premise, it cannot easily succeed and may, in fact, be doomed to fail.

QUESTION

# 4

## ARE YOU AFRAID
## OF FAILING?

As a general rule, none of us like to fail. At school, we never wanted to fail a test. At play, we never wanted to strike out or fall down in the midst of a game. And, between 9 and 5, we work hard to be regarded as a success, not a failure.

But there is a vast and significant difference between simply not wanting to fail and being actively afraid of failing.

Because the entrepreneur or would-be entrepreneur considers all possibilities, the possibility that a venture may not succeed is one of the scenarios which he considered in advance of making the decision to move forward.

If the truth be told, the quintessential entrepreneur doesn't really believe that he is going to fail. He understands that there will be obstacles but he doesn't doubt that he can — and will — overcome them.

Considering the possibility of failure is a necessary prerequisite for success.

Being seriously afraid of failing will most likely lead to failure.

Determine your own attitude about failure. You should simply consider it as a rational possibility, not an inevitable probability. It should not be an outcome that actively frightens you. That is the healthy, productive entrepreneurial perspective.

QUESTION

# 5

## ARE YOU AFRAID
## OF SUCCEEDING?

Fear of failure is a common fear; fear of success sounds almost like a paradox. But, to many, it is as real as the fear of failure. It is clearly a fear that the entrepreneur-to-be cannot afford — since success is the entrepreneur's bottom line.

The fear of success can encompass many problems — and many people in your life:
*Will success spoil me?*
*Will success spoil my children?*
*Will my spouse be able to cope with success?*
*Will my parents be jealous of my success?*
*Will my friends leave me when I'm successful?*
*Will I leave my friends when I'm successful?*
*Will I be able to sustain my success?*

Consciously, no entrepreneur-to-be fears success. Unconsciously, of course, it can be an entirely different and disruptive matter.

The key is to regard success as a well-deserved dividend of your hard work rather than as a lightning bolt which will transform you. Then, when it arrives, it can be comfortably integrated into your life (and your family's life) without altering anyone's basic values.

# 6

# WOULD YOU CONSIDER
# YOURSELF STUBBORN?

Children are often taught that stubbornness is not a virtue. A stubborn child is often regarded as a difficult child. In truth, he should be regarded as a future entrepreneur!

Even in adults, of course, stubbornness can frequently be a vice rather than a virtue. Stubbornness born out of revenge or anger or simply a mean-spirited desire to disrupt someone's objectives is neither useful or healthy.

Stubbornness born out of determination, principle or the certainty that it will lead to improvement can be a valuable trait resulting in positive change.

The true entrepreneur doesn't consider himself stubborn. He simply regards himself as a believer. But, no matter the definition, he often acts stubbornly — usually while resisting an expected or conventional response in favor of an unexpected or unconventional one.

To the entrepreneur, *well-intentioned* stubbornness is a virtue, a catalyst for creative change.

It's the entrepreneur's way of saying no while thinking of a better way to go!

QUESTION

# 7

## DO YOU HAVE
## "STAYING POWER?"

It is no surprise that successful athletes often become successful entrepreneurs. To the good athlete, "staying power" is a reflex.

In baseball, he will keep fouling off pitches until he gets one he can hit. In football, he will keep punching through the opposition until he creates a path to victory. And, in business, he will stick to his "game plan" no matter the obstacles.

If you often find yourself discouraged or battle-weary, even when you know that you're on the right path, your personal brand of "staying power" needs some work.

But if you instinctively hang in there, like the good athlete, confident that everything will work out so long as you don't give up or give in, then you have the magnitude of "staying power" that a successful entrepreneur needs.

Sometimes, "staying power" simply means working harder. At other times, it may mean finding a successful way to beat back the competition. Or it may mean that you have to keep more money than you expected in the business for a longer period than you planned.

In any variation, it means that you have to have the ability and the tenacity to resist the temptation to give up before you've given yourself every reasonable opportunity to make it.

There's no guarantee that you'll make it every time.

But your chances of making it will diminish in proportion to your lack of "staying power."

Therefore, regard "staying power" as an important asset on your personal balance sheet. It can make the difference between success and failure as an entrepreneur.

QUESTION

# 8

# WOULD YOU CONSIDER
# YOURSELF CONFIDENT?

The entrepreneur needs a genuine sense of self-assurance, of confidence . . . in himself, in his plans, in his prospects.

Most importantly, that sense of confidence has to be real.

It cannot be tentative or fabricated. It has to spring from within, from a deep-rooted belief that he is doing the very best that he can — and that that will be good enough to achieve his objectives.

Do you know how easy it is for you to spot a faker, a con man? As the saying goes, you can spot him a mile away!

Virtually everyone who chooses to do business with a new business has that same sense, the ability to distinguish the probable winners from the likely losers.

To be a winner, you have to feel like a winner. Just ask Joe Namath! There was nothing phony about his confidence before the Super Bowl. He believed he was going to win — and he won!

Your confidence will spring from the most valid confidence-creating "secret" of all: The certainty that you have done your homework, planned and prepared for every reasonable eventuality, mastered the details of your new business until they were second nature to you.

If you've done your homework, your confidence will be real.

In turn, everyone will respond positively to you: Your customers, your employees, your creditors, even your competitors.

Everyone likes to be associated with a winner . . . and all winners share a common characteristic: Genuine self-confidence in themselves and their mission.

QUESTION

# 9

# DO YOU THINK
# YOU POSSESS
# LEADERSHIP QUALITIES?

One of the least-known definitions of leadership, according to one popular dictionary, is "to proceed toward one's true purpose." It is an especially appropriate definition for one who is thinking about going into business for himself. Because the ability to lead is an absolute prerequisite for the entrepreneur-to-be.

There are those who lead by directive, and there are those who lead by example.

In the independent business world, where actions truly speak louder than words, the ability to motivate those around you requires active, "hands-on" leadership.

You are going to have to lead by example, for more hours and with greater intensity than you could ever imagine.

You will have to be there — *everywhere* — showing everyone what has to be done and how to do it!

Hopefully, the act of leadership comes comfortably to you. Hopefully, motivating and maximizing the actions of others is a skill you possess in abundance.

If it is not, think of that dictionary definition. The very act of becoming an entrepreneur is a commitment "to proceeding towards one's true purpose." And, while you will undoubtedly be the trail-blazer, it is not a path that you will be traveling alone. You will need the help of everyone around you.

The natural leader expects two results from his leadership: Response and respect.

If you can gain the respect of your constituents — most particularly your customers and your employees — then positive response will follow: You will have devoted employees and satisfied customers. And you will have successfully established the basis for your present — and future — success as an entrepreneur.

QUESTION

# 10

# CAN YOU
# TAKE CONTROL OF
# YOUR LIFE?

One of the most universal reasons for wanting to go into business for oneself is to gain greater control over one's life.

That's the good news.

The bad news is that not everyone has the ability to take control — even when it's something they want to do.

Think about control this way: Imagine that the only place where you can set up your office is in your kitchen, inches away from the refrigerator, the fully-stocked cupboard and the cookie jar. Would you have any serious difficulty getting down to business in that tempting environment? Would you be able to resist all those goodies around you? Would you be able to concentrate on the tasks at hand?

If your answer is "most of the time," then you've got a good handle on your sense of self-discipline.

And self-discipline is really what the concept of control is all about.

As an employee, you were often told what to do — and, in fact, that may have been one of the reasons you began the process of thinking about going into business for yourself.

As an entrepreneur, the only one telling you what to do will be your own inner voice.

Taking control of your life means that (1) you have to be able to hear that voice and (2) you have to have the ability to respond to it.

Not every question in this book carries equal weight; some are obviously more important as determinants than others. This one is one of the "heavier" ones and therefore has only one correct answer.

Can you take control of your life?

In the words of network sportscaster Marv Albert, your answer has to be: *"Yes-s-s-s-s-s!"*

# 11

## CAN YOU
## TAKE CONTROL OF OTHERS?

It's back to the dictionary for this question. The popular definition of control is "to exercise authority or influence" over others. A secondary definition is "restraint or reserve."

To effectively control others — basically, in the context of this question, your employees — you have to have the capacity to balance your sense of authority with a sense of restraint. This will enable you to exercise authority without being heavy-handed.

When it came to the previous question — controlling your own life — you had to be tough on yourself, to impose strong self-discipline upon yourself in the absence of a "boss."

For the purpose of this question, of course, you are the "boss." And, in that role, your objective to keep your employees under control requires a very different set of skills.

Can you balance the carrot and the stick? Have you been a successful parent? Can you exert influence over others without evoking a negative reaction?

To be a successful entrepreneur/boss, you will have to balance the toughness of a drill sergeant with the smoothness of a diplomat. It is not an easy combination to achieve.

In truth, it is a test of your character — one which, as an entrepreneur, you cannot permit yourself to fail.

QUESTION

# 12

## COULD YOU
## HIRE SOMEONE?

Most of us make judgment calls every day of our lives. When we buy an article of clothing. When we select an ear of corn out of a greengrocer's overflowing bin. When we pick a plumber or a lawn care service or even a car.

But none of these judgments are as sensitive as hiring someone who will be working with you in a new enterprise.

That is truly a difficult and critical judgment call.

And judgment is what this question — and its answer — are all about.

For example, there are colleges and universities which heavily weigh grades and SAT scores in making their evaluations of prospective students. Then there are those schools which look more closely at personal essays and teacher recommendations together with an interview with the applicant.

As an entrepreneur/employer, you will have to develop your own formula, your own balance of judgment in the on-going process of hiring people.

Two facts stand out:

One, you will have to hire people — if not at first, certainly eventually. Two, you will have to be right much more often than you are wrong!

Did you have the opportunity to hire others while you were an employee? Did most of your new-hires work out for the best?

That's an easy test, of course, and one (which like most easy tests) may not have any direct application to your new business.

The more important value here is your confidence in your

ability to size up others. And that is most likely an ability of which you already have some self-awareness.

The time and energy of bringing new people into a business, of training them, of inducing them to provide the efficiency you need, can be a costly one. Therefore, you will have to make every effort to bring in good people from the start (and, of course, to create an environment which will encourage them to stay on).

Chances are that you developed considerable "people skills" as an employee.

The certainty is that you will have to continue to develop them as an employer.

QUESTION

# 13

## COULD YOU
## FIRE SOMEONE?

Going into business for yourself is a positive decision — an affirmation of one's ambition and confidence and determination to succeed.

It is, to quote our old friend Marv Albert, a very loud and affirmative "Yes-s-s-s-s!"

But the successful entrepreneur/employer must also have the ability — and the willingness — to say "No."

The prospect of having to dismiss an employee brings to mind that uncomfortable phrase most of us heard as a child: "This is going to hurt me more than it's going to hurt you."

But, like most ancient phrases that have survived the test of time, there is a great deal of truth in that awkward but applicable adage.

An employee who, for one reason or another, doesn't work out becomes a liability both to himself and to the business which employs him.

As an employer, you have an obligation to reduce your liabilities.

As a human being, you have an obligation to help others (without intentionally hurting them in the process).

Often, asking someone to depart from an enterprise will achieve both objectives.

Firing someone will always be an uncomfortable process.

But it is a process which you will inevitably have to deal with as an employer.

One day, sooner or later, you will have to make the decision to fire someone.

Can you do it?

The appropriate answer should be, "Yes . . . if I have to."

So, logically, first you must develop the ability to determine when an employee becomes a liability to your business. You will be surprised to learn that in most instances the answer becomes obvious.

And then you must develop the ability to dismiss someone . . . diplomatically. You will be equally surprised (and relieved) to discover that your about-to-be ex-employee usually knows that you are making the correct decision and will even feel an inner sense of relief — although you would never know it from the unhappy or even hostile reaction you will often suffer at the moment of truth.

QUESTION

# 14

# ARE YOU COMFORTABLE
# WORKING FOR YOURSELF?

As we know, the decision to go into business for yourself evidences a great deal of self-confidence and courage. But, as you consider the possibility of working for yourself, spend a minute reflecting on the most critical ingredient of that new and challenging equation: *Yourself.*

What do you think of your prospective new boss?
Do you like him?
Do you trust him?
Do you like living with him?
What's he really like in a crisis?
Does he make you happy or sad?
What will he be like to work for?

Though these may superficially sound like rhetorical questions, they are really very critical, down-to-the-core questions. Because if you're going to be working for yourself, you've really got to like and trust the person you'll be working for . . . yourself!

To be comfortable working *for* yourself, you've got to be comfortable *with* yourself.

QUESTION

# 15

# ARE YOU COMFORTABLE
# WORKING WITH OTHERS?

A common characteristic of entrepreneurs, according to studies, is that as children they were often characterized as "loners." They could typically get along by themselves if they had to or, in many instances, when they chose to. Perhaps, at one time, you were characterized in that fashion.

At times, that ability can be a strength. For example, when it comes to such qualities as initiative and imagination.

It can, of course, also be a limitation.

*No man is an island, least of all a would-be entrepreneur.*

Unless you're going to be in a one-man business (and even then, of course, you will be dealing with a whole universe of other people), you will have to be part of a team.

As the entrepreneur/employer, you will be the leader of the team.

Even as the leader, you will have to be comfortable working with others.

If the leader of the pack hesitates, the members of the pack become uncertain, uncomfortable and, ultimately, unsuccessful.

So here again you have to make certain that you're working with a positive: *That your decision to go into business for yourself was not a decision to be in business by yourself.*

QUESTION

# 16

## ARE YOU CURIOUS?

Curiosity may have killed the cat, but it certainly keeps the soul of the entrepreneur alive . . . nine times over and then some!

We've never met a successful entrepreneur who wasn't curious . . . about his business, about other businesses, about the world in general!

Curiosity is one of the essential self-propulsion fuels for the entrepreneur-to-be.

He'll clip newspaper articles, jot down questions, search for answers.

He listens carefully and constantly is on the prowl for sources and resources which are unique and unusual.

Curiosity means searching, acknowledging that you don't know it all, suspecting that there might be a wonderful and useful surprise hidden around the next corner.

The typical entrepreneur has been curious for most of his life — and certainly most of his adult life.

Curiosity, of course, takes many shapes and forms. The computer consultant will have one dimension of curiosity and the owner of a fast-food franchise an entirely different one.

While the computer consultant is working on a new software program into the pre-dawn hours, the fast-food franchisee might be reading a report about how others are operating similar businesses halfway around the world.

Perhaps the most useful definition of an entrepreneur's curiosity is that it is a combination of brainstorming with yourself while never being satisfied with your own body of knowledge.

Does that describe you?

# 17

## ARE YOU CREATIVE?

Creativity, like curiosity, has entirely distinct meanings within the entrepreneurial universe.

For a restaurant owner, it might be coming up with a wonderful name for his chef's newest recipe.

For an auto parts dealer, it might simply be deciding to open his store half an hour earlier each weekday, to accommodate commuters.

For the owner of a dancing school, it might be to select a bright new color for the school's uniform leotards.

Creativity, in the entrepreneur's definition, means the constant desire to put a fresh new face on your business — to keep it vibrant and exciting — to prevent it from becoming stale.

It doesn't mean writing a great novel, discovering a new star or perfecting a cure for the common cold.

For the entrepreneur, creativity is a much more immediate, pragmatic expression.

It is a commitment to keeping his business fresh and alive.

As a result, his success, like his business, will have a constantly fresh and exciting face!

QUESTION

# 18

## WOULD YOU CONSIDER
## YOURSELF PASSIONATE?

Think of Bob Newhart. Would you consider him passionate? Probably not.

He started out many years ago as an accountant and today he is perhaps TV's most consistent and successful situation comedy performer. In his laid-back manner, he certainly doesn't appear passionate. But you'd better believe that he is *very* passionate — about delivering the very best performance he can each and every time that camera light comes on!

That's the kind of passion an entrepreneur needs: *The passion to do his best . . . and then do even better the next time out!*

The passion to succeed.

The passion to create.

The passion to build a business and a life which will bring him (and his loved ones) satisfaction.

You don't have to wear your entrepreneurial heart on your sleeve.

But you do have to feel it in your bones.

You have to care.

You have to feel committed.

You have to wake up each morning wanting to make today just a little bit better than yesterday.

Think about Bob Newhart. And if you find yourself smiling when he comes to mind, all's well with your PQ (Passion Quotient)!

QUESTION

# 19

# WOULD YOU CONSIDER
# YOURSELF EMOTIONAL?

Throughout this book, we've accentuated the positive because the decision to become an entrepreneur is an affirmation, a positive and productive decision. Therefore, at all times, the entrepreneur has to be on guard against negative intrusions, forces which might get in the way of his progress (and profit).

Being passionate, as we just discussed, is positive.
One dictionary describes passion as "boundless enthusiasm."

Being emotional, as we're about to discuss, is negative.
That same dictionary describes emotional as "agitation of the passions or sensibilities."

The entrepreneur, in the ordinary course of business, is going to have to deal with enough normal agitation; therefore, creating additional and unnecessary agitation is not a useful exercise.

So, if you know that you tend to be emotional, become acutely aware of that tendancy — and try to check it before it gets in the way of your business.

The symptoms are obvious: If, for example, you get angry when someone slips into a parking space ahead of you ... or picks up the last newspaper on the rack ... or hangs up on you before you believe that the conversation is ended. If these examples sound familiar, you *are* emotional. And, as an entrepreneur-to-be, you have to be twice as hard on yourself to keep your emotions in check before they escalate into a deficit on your personal and business balance sheet.

QUESTION

# 20

## WOULD YOU CONSIDER YOURSELF RATIONAL?

This is the flip side of emotion. And whereas you should keep your emotions in check, you are encouraged to develop your rational skills.

There's an old saying on Wall Street that the successful stock trader never "falls in love" with a stock. When the facts indicate that it's time to sell, he sells — even though he may have an emotional attachment to the stock.

Because an entrepreneur has to have a high level of enthusiasm and belief in his product or service (typically "falling in love" with every new item or idea), there is the on-going danger that his rational side can be overruled by emotion.

To sidestep this trap, the rational entrepreneur has to be ready to stop marketing an unsuccessful product . . . to cut back his plans to expand into the neighboring town . . . to give up an idea he was certain was going to work . . . once the hard facts suggest otherwise.

If being emotional can be compared to over-eating, then being rational can be compared to working out.

As an entrepreneur, you've got to work out your logical, sensible "mental muscles" every day — to keep yourself and your business in good shape.

QUESTION

# 21

## WOULD YOU CONSIDER
## YOURSELF OBJECTIVE?

Words are often like colors, suggesting the mood or the environment surrounding a situation. Think about these words: *Fair. Reasonable. Thoughtful.* If they were colors, they would be considered so-called neutral colors. As a frame of reference, they reflect the objectivity which an entrepreneur must bring to countless situations.

As an entrepreneur, you will frequently find yourself the eye of a hurricane: *When workers argue . . . when customers have a complaint . . . when suppliers are making unexpected demands of you.*

During these often-charged moments, the entrepreneur must take caution to act in a calm and reflective manner. He doesn't want to fan the flames of a dispute; rather, he wants to dampen a problem before it becomes a three-alarm disaster that threatens to explode out of control.

As the entrepreneur in the eye of the storm, you will have to consider all of the elements without prejudice or anger or a pre-established viewpoint. To keep your workers, your customers and your suppliers in your good graces, you have to continually win their respect.

And during those inflammatory occasions when a spark can either be extinguished or ignited, you will have to convince all of the participants in the dispute of your objectivity.

At these moments, those three neutral qualities we spoke of become your strength, your secret weapon: *Fairness. Reasonableness. Thoughtfulness.* Together, they are the source — and the strength — of your objectivity.

QUESTION

# 22

# ARE YOU AFRAID OF
# TAKING RISKS?

Millions of happy and productive people go through life playing it safe. They establish a "comfort zone" for themselves and rarely operate outside of its . . . well, comfortable . . . limits.

Typically, these are not the sort of people who make the decision to go into business for themselves.

Yet, of course, becoming an entrepreneur is not synonomous with behaving like a daredevil!

By definition, an entrepreneur consciously takes risks.

The very act of beginning a business is a risk.

The typical entrepreneur makes hundreds of judgment calls each week, many of which contain risky elements.

For the entrepreneur to be able to operate without excessive doubt or despair, he has to be comfortable with the concept of risk-taking.

And, just as importantly, his confidence has to be shared by his family.

So, make certain that you are comfortable with *rational* risk-taking (as opposed to gambling, which is the subject of the next question) . . . and be sure that your family can comfortably sustain the stress of living well beyond the range of the "comfort zone" of most people.

QUESTION

# 23

# DO YOU KNOW THE DIFFERENCE BETWEEN A RISK AND A GAMBLE?

What's the difference between a risk and a gamble?

A high-wire circus performer who works with a net is taking a risk. One who works without one is taking a gamble!

*You will not be able to succeed as an entrepreneur if you cannot instinctively differentiate between a risk and a gamble.*

If your entrepreneurial risks — business judgments, really — are based on persuasive, objective data, you will be operating from one of the successful entrepreneur's classic strengths: To see where others can't, to be willing to reach where others haven't, to open doors where others have walked away.

If you have the undisciplined instincts of a gambler — willing to "bet the farm" on a speculative piece of unreliable or uncertain or unsubstantiated information — then you will fail as an entrepreneur because, like the second high-wire performer in the example, there will be no net to break your fall.

Sure, sometimes, like a good poker player, you will find yourself in the position of having to "bluff" your way through a situation.

If bluffing — and often finding yourself on the brink of losing everything you own or value — is a way of life for you, then thinking of becoming an entrepreneur is a dangerous decision for you.

To be a prudent, successful, long-term entrepreneur, you have to know (and appreciate and value) the difference between taking a sensible risk and taking a senseless gamble.

Keep in mind the most fundamental truth of all, well-known to innkeepers in Las Vegas and Atlantic City: Eventually, gamblers *always* lose!

QUESTION

# 24

# ARE YOU A SINGLE OR OLDEST CHILD?

Were you the oldest child in your house, asked to take on responsibilities your younger brothers or sisters were spared? Or were you a single child, without siblings to share your thoughts (and toys and clothes) with?

In either event, your childhood memories might be marked by some less-than-perfect moments.

But today, as you are contemplating the prospect of going into business for yourself, the fact that you are a single or oldest child might well be an advantage you have simply by accident of birth.

Single or oldest children are often precocious, ahead of their peers because of the circumstances of their position within their family.

Oldest children are often given responsibilities early in life — much as entrepreneurs take on responsibilities at the beginning of launching a new business.

Single children often turn to adults as companions because of the unavailability of kids their own age at home — much as the entrepreneur has to become sophisticated in a hurry once he switches from the role of employee to that of employer.

Obviously, oldest or single children are not assured of success — and the youngest child in a family of six can write the greatest success story imaginable.

But, historically, oldest or single children have some natural advantages as adults — in terms of accepting and managing responsibilities.

So, then, this question is really one to make oldest or single children who are thinking about becoming entrepreneurs feel better: Your parents may have done you a favor which is about to pay off!

QUESTION

# 25

# WHAT DID YOUR FATHER
# DO FOR A LIVING?

Was your father a mailman, a lawyer or a salesman? A factory worker, a teacher or an independent businessman?

It's not news, of course, that the environment in which we grow up has a great deal to do with the way we act when we grow up. The values of the entrepreneur-to-be often took root while he was still negotiating for an extra dollar a week allowance!

If you grew up in a household where the breadwinner, for instance, was a civil servant, someone who valued "security" above all else and took great comfort in the fact that he could never lose his job because of his guaranteed tenure, perhaps that sense of security was passed on to you. If so, that hereditary state of mind probably did not encourage your entrepreneurial spirit.

On the other hand, it's entirely possible that someone growing up in that environment could question the trade-off of security for, say, the absence of significant challenges and therefore develop into an aggressive entrepreneur — determined to establish that the only genuine "security" is the security which one creates for himself.

It is, however, more likely that entrepreneurial inclinations are developed earlier and stronger in families where the head of the household is not a complete stranger to risk or uncertainty.

In that sort of atmosphere, both the pros and cons of the risks inherent in becoming an entrepreneur are experienced — and then selectively adapted when the child joins the workforce.

So, if your dad was a salesman or a small retail storeowner, you have the advantage of knowing what life without a guaranteed pay check is all about.

Living with that experience could have turned you off on the whole idea of going into business for yourself.

However, the odds are that the experience is one of the unconscious positive factors propelling you towards the difficult but dauntless world of the entrepreneur.

QUESTION

# 26

# WHAT DID YOUR MOTHER DO FOR A LIVING?

More women than ever in history are in the workforce today — both as employees and entrepreneurs.

But, of course, that wasn't always the case — even as recently as 25 years ago.

If you grew up in a home where your mother was the traditional "homemaker," then you were raised in an entirely normal and healthy household.

If you grew up in a home where your mother was part of the workforce, either as an employee or as an entrepreneur, then you were raised in a home where you unconsciously knew that "anything is possible."

Depending on your age (say, if you're over 30), growing up in such a home was really the experience of being raised in a home where classic, historic roles were challenged — where your mother was more than the PTA profile of a "homemaker."

And growing up in a home where "anything is possible" is obviously a wonderful place for an entrepreneur-to-be to grow up.

Because if entrepreneurs share one common motto, it would be: "Anything is possible!"

QUESTION

# 27

## WHAT DID YOU WANT TO BE
## WHEN YOU GREW UP?

Did you set up a lemonade stand on the street in front of your house during the summer you turned ten? Did you have a newspaper route as a child, or would you drop everything for the chance to spend an afternoon in your father's office?

These are all early indications of the sense of direction which we take later in life.

No one seriously expects a nine or 15-year-old to chart his life's passage, but early signs of later developments are often true indicators.

If math came easily to you, you might have decided early on to become an engineer or if collecting the money from your paper route — and keeping the profits for yourself — turned you on, you might have decided early on that being in business for yourself was the best idea in the world.

Were you ambitious as a child or lazy? Were you eager to "do something" or willing to stand around and watch others "do something?" Did your family talk about business around the dinner table — and seem to enjoy it?

Obviously, selling Scout cookies or tossing newspapers on neighborhood lawns isn't a sure sign of becoming an entrepreneur as an adult — but it is an early indication that you might be one of those who will achieve personal satisfaction by making things happen for — and on — your own account.

QUESTION

# 28

## DO YOU THINK OF
## YOURSELF AS "GROWN-UP?"

We'll admit it up front: There is no black-or-white answer to this question. The answer isn't an absolute but a balance — the balance between maturity and innocence.

Yes, it's important for the entrepreneur-to-be to feel "grown-up" — in the sense that he is willing to accept responsibility and be held accountable for his own actions (or inactions).

BUT ... and it's really a big "but" ...

It's equally important for the entrepreneur-to-be not to fully "grow up!"

What's that?

We mean it: If "growing up" means the loss of innocence, of being open to all sorts of new ideas, of being willing to explore new horizons, then it's best for the entrepreneurial candidate never to fully grow up. Because this dimension of open-mindedness and even playfulness is essential to the creativity of the entrepreneur.

So, what's the "right" answer: Think of yourself as "grown-up" in terms of handling responsibilities ... but never fully "grown-up" so that you might miss opportunities which are unavailable to those who equate "growing up" with having a closed mind!

QUESTION

# 29

# DO YOU HAVE THE ABILITY TO SET GOALS?

Are you familiar with those memo pads which you can buy in any stationery store, the one with the bold headline: THINGS TO DO TODAY?

Do you buy them and use them ... or have you bought them, and then been afraid to fill them in?

Whereas the immediately preceeding question (about growing up) had no absolute answers, this question has only one absolutely appropriate answer: AS AN ENTREPRENEUR-TO-BE, YOU MUST HAVE THE ABILITY TO SET GOALS!!!

You cannot even think about beginning a business with vague objectives: *I'd like to make it work ... If I can just earn five hundred dollars a month more than I'm earning now ... With a couple of good breaks, everything'll work out, I'm sure.*

Nothing about running a business is vague; everyone wants to get exactly what they're paying for.

Similarly, nothing about beginning a business is vague.

YOU MUST KNOW WHAT YOU WANT ... YOU MUST BE ABLE TO SPELL OUT THOSE OBJECTIVES ... AND YOU MUST BE ABLE TO SET GOALS — FOR YOUR CUSTOMERS, YOUR EMPLOYEES, YOUR SUPPLIERS — AND YOURSELF!

QUESTION

# 30

# DO YOU HAVE A TRACK RECORD FOR ACHIEVING GOALS?

Although we just finished saying it on the preceeding page, it bears repeating: THE ENTREPRENEUR-TO-BE MUST HAVE THE ABILITY TO SET GOALS!

The follow-up question ... this question ... isn't quite as simple.

If your answer to this question is "yes" because your goals have always been modest, then it's not necessarily a comforting response.

If you've always set high standards for yourself and, more often than not, been able to reach them, then your "yes" is very encouraging.

And if yours is a mixed answer, there is nothing to be discouraged about.

The very best hitters in baseball only hit .350 — which means that they fail to get a hit six-and-a-half out of every ten at-bats.

That's not an equivalent average for business success, but it does remind us that no one achieves objectives every time out.

But as an entrepreneur, you will constantly have to set goals — and, therefore, the more often you have achieved them in the past, the greater the probability that you will be able to do so in the future.

QUESTION

# 31

# DO YOU HAVE THE ABILITY
# TO CONCENTRATE?

Do you like to solve problems? Do you enjoy being presented with a challenge and then spending the necessary time and energy to meet it? Or do you walk away from a problem or a challenge if you can't solve it or meet it within the first 30 seconds?

Solving problems and meeting challenges are everyday occurrences in the entrepreneurial world; there isn't an entrepreneur alive who hasn't experienced at least one problem or challenge during each day that he's been in business for himself.

And the only way to solve a problem or meet a challenge is to concentrate on the issue at hand.

A guess — at best! — will provide you with the right answer only 50% of the time and a casual, easy-does-it approach will guarantee you the *wrong* answer close to 100% of the time!

Therefore, as an entrepreneur, you must have — or develop — the ability to concentrate.

QUESTION

# 32

## ARE YOU

## IN GOOD HEALTH?

The best advice before starting a diet or fitness program is to check the state of your health with a physician.

The same advice is at the top of the list for entrepreneurs-to-be.

What kind of hours does a new businessperson keep?
*Irregular.*
How does a new businessperson eat?
*Irregularly.*
What is a new businessperson guaranteed?
*Irregularity* — of time and habits.

Therefore, like any long-distance runner about to begin a test of endurance, make certain that you are in good physical condition.

If you've recently had a medical check-up, were given a clean bill of health and nothing has changed, terrific. Ready, set, go!

But if you haven't had a recent medical examination and/or you have some questions about your current state of health, then do not even contemplate going into business for yourself until you've received a medical seal of approval.

Good health is a *must* prescription for good business!

QUESTION

# 33

## DO YOU HAVE A HIGH ENERGY LEVEL?

We've just noted the importance of the state of your health — but not all healthy people have high levels of energy.

And energy — or stamina or resilience — is something which the entrepreneur must have in abundance.

You know the old truth about performers — that they're always "on" — whether they're on stage or off-stage.

In a manner of speaking, as an entrepreneur, you will always be "on" — in a state of energized animation — for as many hours each day as you devote to your business.

You will have to be "on" when there are no customers in your store (or else your employees will get down).

You will have to be "on" when your banker tells you that he can't meet your requirements this time (or else he won't even consider your application next time).

These examples, and countless others, demand that you retain a high energy level all day long, day after day.

Some of us have "natural" high energy levels; others of us, like boxers getting ready for a bout, have to develop it until we are strong enough to go as many rounds as it takes.

The entrepreneur never knows how many rounds it will take — and therefore the entrepreneur has to build up his energy level to championship rank.

QUESTION

# 34

# DO YOU HAVE THE ABILITY TO "RE-CHARGE YOUR BATTERIES?"

We were just speaking of boxers, so we'll keep the thought going. Even the best-conditioned fighter will begin to tire during the closing rounds of a battle. The losers are unable to find the energy they need to win. The winners are able to re-charge their batteries during the one-minute break between rounds.

It is equally important for a hard-working, hard-driving entrepreneur to find the time and to develop the ability to recharge his batteries.

For some, meditation does the trick.

For others, a quick catnap on the office sofa.

For still others, a long weekend in the country.

Whatever your favorite formula, you will have to find one that works for you.

It is essential for the entrepreneur to be awake and alert and alive during working hours.

And it is impossible for anyone to be in that state without a break.

The trick is to make each break work for you, in your fashion so that when you need the energy you will have it!

QUESTION

# 35

## DO YOU TRUST YOURSELF?

As an entrepreneur, you will have to place your trust in many other people — ranging from your accountant to the overnight cleaning crew.

You will be unable to comfortably trust anyone unless you trust the most important person of all — yourself!

Therefore, make sure of this:
*That you trust your ability to make decisions.*
*That you trust your creativity, commitment and courage.*
*And, most importantly of all, that you trust your instincts!*

You *have* to trust yourself before you can begin to trust others — which just so happens to be the subject of our next question.

QUESTION

# 36

## DO YOU TRUST OTHERS?

Unless you trust yourself, you will be unable to trust others. And it is essential for the entrepreneur to trust others.

One of the classic reasons that a new business fails is because the new business owner — the entrepreneur — is unable to delegate.

The reason that he is unable to delegate duties and responsibilities is because he doesn't have enough trust in others to enable them to take on these duties and responsibilities — even though, in the end, he would be the primary beneficiary!

Therefore, the entrepreneur who has the ability to trust others has a major advantage in the management — and eventual growth — of his business.

A business cannot grow if its entire strength depends on the presence of one person.

It is alright for the *direction* of the business to be dependent on a single vision; it is impossible for the *operation* of the business to be dependent on a single person.

Therefore, it is imperative that the entrepreneur has the ability to trust others. And for the strongest and simplest reason of all: He *needs* others to achieve the success he seeks!

QUESTION

# 37

# ARE YOU INTIMIDATED
# BY LAWYERS?

Lawyers, in a sense, are no different from plumbers or the counter personnel at McDonald's: They are in a service business and need satisfied customers to stay in business.

You probably haven't considered attorneys in that light — and, frankly, that's the way many members of the legal profession prefer it.

But as an entrepreneur, you have to regard your lawyer as someone there to provide you with a basic service: Providing you with the legal documents — and legal counsel — you need to meet the legal requirements for starting a business and staying in business.

Therefore, obviously, a skillful and responsive lawyer is a key player on your team. You will need a lawyer with whom you are comfortable and one who is supportive of your objectives.

Just as "family medicine" has become a popular specialty among physicians eager to get back to basics, "small business law" has become a popular — and profitable — area for lawyers.

Recommendations from successful independent businessmen in your community are probably the most reliable source for locating lawyers sympathetic to, and effective on behalf of, entrepreneurs.

Don't let the wall full of degrees and bar admissions intimidate you. The bottom line is that you're the customer.

QUESTION

# 38

## ARE YOU INTIMIDATED
## BY ACCOUNTANTS?

Whereas some attorneys intentionally set out to intimidate others, accountants manage to intimidate outsiders simply because of the nature of their work: Endless sheets filled with infinite numbers designed to meet the requirements of impossible statutes, laws and rulings.

Just as an operating room doesn't intimidate a good surgeon, all of the tax and accounting complications don't intimidate working accountants.

The trick for the entrepreneur is to find an accountant who will share his confidence and knowledge in a useful and understandable manner.

Numbers, not words, are the bottom line language of business — and you will have to become fluent in that language if your business is to prosper.

Again, recommendations from reliable sources are your best bet. Setting up the books and meeting the tax requirements for a small business demand a special commitment from accountants who *enjoy* that sort of work.

Your challenge will be to find an accountant who will regard you as an opportunity rather than a burden.

# 39

## ARE YOU INTIMIDATED
## BY BANKERS?

The truth is that on some level *everyone* is intimidated by bankers, from the treasurer of a Fortune 500 company looking for a multi-million dollar line of credit to the newlywed couple looking for a first mortgage.

Again, it's simply a matter of how you regard bankers.

Banks have one primary product to sell: Money.

They can only make money if they make their money work.

The difference between bankers and other sellers of goods is that, eventually, bankers want you to return their product!

The entrepreneur has to present a banker with two products of his own: His homework and his credibility.

*Homework* simply means what it says: Preparing complete, almost over-bearing documentation about the financial health and prospects of your business. Bankers take comfort in complete paperwork; it provides them with the evidence they need to make a decision.

*Credibility* means being honest with your banker. Don't tell him you're going to net $50,000 when that's the high side of your projections. He would rather hear $35,000 — and be pleasantly surprised. But if he expects $50,000 and you come back with $35,000 (no matter how healthy a number it is), he will be disappointed, perhaps even angry. Angry bankers are not helpful to a beginning — or even an established — business!

More and more, major banks are setting up departments to accommodate small business. But there are also many small banks — sometimes characterized as "hungry" banks — who have long-standing policies of encouraging new businesses in their town.

No matter which kind of bank you choose, remember the fundamentals: If you do your homework and play it straight, the chances of being able to "buy" their product — money — will be significantly increased.

It may be hard to believe but the banks need you as much as you need them.

QUESTION

# 40.

# ARE YOU INTIMIDATED
# BY THE IRS?

Even if you go into business for yourself without partners, you *will* have a partner from Day One: Uncle Sam!

It will begin when you have to apply to your regional IRS center for an employer identification number (the business equivalent of a Social Security number) — and your relationship with the tax authorities will intensify from that day forth.

Make yourself two promises — and then make sure to keep them! — and your relationship with your partner the IRS should not bring you any discomfort.

(1) *Keep meticulous records.* Keep a record of everything which affects your business, from tipping a deliveryman to getting each employee to provide you with a withholding slip. The IRS relies on records, and makes it your burden to maintain complete and accurate ones. If you do so, should a problem ever arise, the IRS will be much more inclined to see things your way.

(2) *Never be late.* Cleanliness may be next to Godliness, but to the IRS there is nothing more important than timeliness! Always file on time — and always get a "Proof of Mailing" from your local post office.

Then, with any luck, the IRS will prove to be the best partner of all: Your "silent" partner!

QUESTION

# 41

# CAN YOU GIVE UP
# THE SECURITY OF A
# REGULAR PAYCHECK?

Security, for most of us, is represented by the regularly scheduled receipt of our paycheck. If we are doing our job, and our employer is solvent, then our paycheck should arrive with the certainty of daybreak. Like the rising sun, it will be there, where it is supposed to be, when it is supposed to be there.

For the start-up entrepreneur, that security blanket will probably be unavailable — and, for many, that is among the most difficult adjustments of all in the process of beginning a business.

During the months of organizing a business, before it becomes operational, there will be no paycheck — unless you manage to remain steadily employed during this period or unless you are backed by investors who have scheduled a regular draw for you.

The obvious fall-back, of course, is for the start-up entrepreneur to have sufficient funds on hand to carry him through this payless period.

That's the sensible, rational solution.

But this question really deals with the psychological impact and implications of living without a steady paycheck.

Will you be able to get past Fridays without receiving a paycheck? Will you panic at the prospect of payless paydays? Will your family?

You will in all likelihood have to — so it's a question worth considering.

Like a good Scout, you will have to be prepared for this uncomfortable, if temporary, experience.

If all goes well, this payless period will simply be the lull before the storm — of rising income, increasing profits and joyful confirmation that giving up the security of your regular paycheck was the best move you ever made.

QUESTION

# 42

## WHAT DOES MONEY
## REPRESENT TO YOU?

You've read the magazine stories and newspaper articles, the ones in which ambitious, upwardly-mobile people earning significant incomes talk about what money means to them. Invariably, they will tell the reporter that money is the *only* way of "keeping score," of concretely tracking their success.

That is a dangerous point of view for the emerging entrepreneur.

The most successful entrepreneurs will tell you that if you're going into business *simply* to make money, your chances of success are not encouraging.

Money is a valid reason for going into business — but if it is your overriding objective, then some re-thinking is in order.

Most entrepreneurs report that they went into business for themselves because of their confidence in themselves and their confidence that their business would prove useful to their customers.

In time, if their confidence was justified, their business would prosper.

These successful entrepreneurs never confused the horse and the cart.

They instinctively knew that the horse (the entrepreneur's energy and confidence) came before the cart (profits, the product of that energy and confidence).

If all goes well, the entrepreneur's cart will eventually overflow. It doesn't have a chance unless the entrepreneur concentrates on the horse rather than the cart!

QUESTION

# 43

## COULD YOU LIVE WITHOUT MONEY IF YOU HAD TO?

The emerging entrepreneur has to be ready for the uncertain future he is about to enter. The only certainty is that there will be surprises ahead. One of the biggest surprises will be finding yourself without any money coming in whatsoever.

We've already talked about the ability to live without a regular paycheck.

But now we're talking about living WITHOUT MONEY, period.

*No money coming in this week, next week — or the week after!*

It sounds harsh and, in all truth, it is harsh.

It's like having a stack of chips at the roulette table; every time the wheel turns and your number doesn't come up, you have to give up a couple of more chips — so long as you intend to stay in the game. And no one is there to replace the chips you're giving up.

That is a pretty accurate representation of the start-up period of a new business: No income for the entrepreneur . . . and a series of circumstances that keep begging for more chips.

The only way to survive this period is to be prepared for it — and that means being extremely conservative: If you expect no income for three months, have at least six to nine months of available cash on hand to carry you through. If you expect to be able to take money out of your business within a month, have two to four months of "ready reserve" on hand.

We're not speaking of total assets in this context, just cash on hand. Your total assets will have to be significantly greater than these examples.

*The question:* Could you live without money?

*The answer:* You will probably have to.

*The solution:* Make certain to have enough chips on hand that will carry you through the game until your number — your ability to take money out of your new business — comes up.

## QUESTION

# 44

# CAN YOU WRITE CLEARLY?

Remember the essay you had to write to get into college? Or that classic composition which we were all asked to write back in grade school: "How I Spent My Summer Vacation?"

Hopefully, neither assignment gave you serious difficulty.

At times, as a start-up entrepreneur, you're going to feel like a professional writer: More people than you can imagine will want to get something from you "in writing."

And you will have to be able to express yourself clearly: You will have to get your message across in an effective and understandable style.

Business writing can be compared to composing a headline. Think of the best headlines you've read. They capture the essence of a story in a few words: With strength, simplicity and directness.

That's a wonderful formula for successful business writing — from writing internal memos to drafting outside loan requests: Be strong, simple and direct.

Write well, build a successful business — and you'll be able to have more summer (and winter) vacations than ever. Best of all, you won't have to write about them!

QUESTION

# 45

# ARE YOU AFRAID OF
# SPEAKING IN PUBLIC?

Did you know that Johnny Carson still gets nervous before he steps out on stage — as do many of our popular performers?

As an entrepreneur, you probably will not have to make regular television appearances. But, as you build your business, you will probably have reasonably regular occasions to speak to a diverse group of "publics."

Your bank's loan committee is a public; your customers are a public; a trade association is a public. Thus, you will have to equip yourself to be comfortable and effective in public situations.

Making your audience laugh is not what successful public speaking is all about; making an audience comfortable is.

If you're confident about your subject and determined to share it with directness and thoughtfulness, you'll be OK. In fact, you'll be terrific.

Don't memorize your thoughts . . . just organize them with sincerity and intelligence.

And remember the most comforting truth of all: *Your audience wants to hear what you have to say!*

QUESTION

# 46

## DO YOU HAVE THE
## ABILITY TO LISTEN?

What's something most of us have the equipment to do — and often cannot do well?

To listen!

Successful entrepreneurs have developed the art of listening.

Take this example in a business situations: You can *hear* the customer's complaint easily enough; it's loud and persistent. But you decide to *listen,* as well: "The set broke as soon as we got it home, *but none of your employees would take our problem seriously."*

By listening, you got past the sound and fury of the complaint and learned what the customer is *really* angry about: Not being taken seriously. As soon as you tell him that you *are* taking his problem very seriously, you will be halfway to a satisfactory resolution. And all because you listened!

As an entrepreneur, you will have to develop the skill of listening. By doing so, you will be in a position to receive — and, therefore, deal with — information much earlier than those who don't take the time to listen.

Even in this satellite age, old-fashioned listening is still the most effective and reliable grapevine of all.

QUESTION

# 47

---

## DO YOU ENJOY SELLING?

---

A very successful store has an enormous sign at its front door:
*Rule No. 1: The customer is always right.*
*Rule No. 2: When in doubt, refer to Rule No. 1.*

Of course, in real life, the customer is not always right — but that's not the point.

The point is that a successful salesperson always keeps the customer in mind — and the real point is that *every entrepreneur is a salesperson.* Not only is he a salesperson — but he's selling all the time!

Therefore, it follows that the entrepreneur-to-be has to enjoy the process of selling.

Before you decided to become an entrepreneur, you were a customer.

Think of the most successful sales people you dealt with. They probably all had one common characteristic: You weren't aware when they were selling. Rather, you were probably taken in by their sincerity and helpfulness — and the sense that they really believed in and liked the product or service which they represented.

If you are able to combine the characteristics of your favorite salesperson/role model with the two "rules" at the beginning of this question, you will be in good shape: Because the simple truth is that for as long as you're in business, you will be selling.

QUESTION

# 48

# DO YOU HAVE THE ABILITY
# TO MOTIVATE OTHERS?

Did you ever coach a sports team or direct a school play? Did you ever run for office or organize a fund-raising event? Do you make people feel good about themselves?

If you answered yes to any of these questions, then you have an advantage as an emerging entrepreneur.

By definition, an entrepreneur is self-motivated: He has the ability to get himself going, to believe, to perform, to excel!

In practice, the entrepreneur must have — or develop — the ability to motivate others: To get *them* going!

Your business cannot succeed unless you are able to motivate your employees to constantly do their best.

You will have to be their coach — their psychiatrist — their cheerleader — and their leader by example.

As a successful entrepreneur, you will have to do for others what you do for yourself: *Motivate them to be willing to climb the highest mountain by convincing them that nothing beats the view from the top!*

QUESTION

# 49

# DO YOU HAVE THE ABILITY TO BOUNCE BACK FROM SETBACKS?

Have you ever been a door-to-door salesperson? If you have, then you know how many doors get slammed in your face before one stays open long enough for you to make your pitch.

The successful door-to-door salesperson knows that he can't afford to take each closed door personally — or else he wouldn't be able to stay in business.

Similarly, the new entrepreneur has to accept that a lot of doors are going to close on him — and that, like the door-to-door salesperson, he will simply have to move on — if he wants to stay in business!

One entrepreneur who had many slammed in his face early in his career devised this little trick. He simply decided, each time he was shut out, "It's *their* problem . . . it's *their* missed opportunity." And he promptly went on to the next prospect — without feeling sorry for himself or missing a beat.

That may not work for you but you will have to learn to understand that setbacks are a regular part of business (especially a new business) — and that you will simply have to get past them to move ahead.

QUESTION

# 50

## CAN YOU DISTINGUISH
## BETWEEN A "SETBACK"
## AND A "DEFEAT?"

We've just spoken of setbacks — and the need to develop the capacity to move past them, on to the next opportunity.

The bad news is that, in business, there are many setbacks.

The good news is that there are very few outright defeats.

Losing a prime piece of land on the best intersection in town to a higher bidder is a defeat.

Being delayed by the zoning board in building on it is a setback.

Setbacks are almost always temporary — and can very often be overcome with imagination and determination.

Defeats may not always be permanent but they are usually so difficult to overcome or overturn that the pragmatic entrepreneur knows when to back off and accept the loss.

Defeats are unhappy endings.

Setbacks, once overcome, however, can lead to new beginnings.

The successful entrepreneur must be able to make the distinction between them so that he doesn't waste his time and money on lost causes — and does invest them on recoverable opportunities!

# 51

## CAN YOU HONESTLY ASSESS YOUR WEAKNESSES?

Have you ever admitted — just to yourself — that you *couldn't* do something?

As an entrepreneur, you will have to recognize that there are some things which you can't do as well as others.

You will have to acknowledge your weaknesses so that you can derive strength from them.

For example, if you hate balancing the books, you have to make certain to have a good bookkeeper or accountant in place.

Or if you're planning to open a restaurant but your favorite place is in the kitchen rather than at the door, then you have to make extra certain to hire a terrific maitre d'.

Often, it is difficult for an entrepreneur to honestly assess his weaknesses.

He believes that he decided to go into business because of his personal strengths — and therefore he is unable or unwilling to even consider his weaknesses.

That level of business blindness can be dangerous to your business health.

To avoid it, you're going to have to learn to level with yourself.

QUESTION

# 52

## CAN YOU HONESTLY
## ASSESS YOUR STRENGTHS?

Compared to the last question — which is difficult for all of us — you might think that this one is easy. The surprise, from the entrepreneur's point of view, is that, in some ways, this is the more difficult question of the two.

There is a natural tendency for confident people (such as entrepreneurs) to over-estimate their abilities. Sometimes, this can work well. Sometimes, it can cause problems.

Think of the runner in a baseball game who is confident of his speed and tries to stretch a single into a double — and is thrown out. He probably is, in fact, a good runner but, in those particular circumstances, he over-estimated his abilities — and was thrown out!

Similarly, the entrepreneur has to be careful not to over-estimate his strengths. They have to be weighed against the particular circumstances of each event.

It is an ever-changing judgment, a constantly measured response.

The successful entrepreneur can determine that successful balance of taking a strong lead without getting picked off base!

QUESTION

# 53

## WOULD YOU CHARACTERIZE
## YOURSELF AS DECISIVE?

This is a true story: Once upon a time, there was a very important banker who was constantly besieged by loan requests from important clients. He dealt with each request in exactly the same way: He would open a file and let the application sit. From time to time, of course, he would be asked about the status of the application — and he was always ready with the same answer: "It's still pending."

*If that banker had been an entrepreneur, he would have been out of business in a week!*

At the beginning of this book, we characterized the emerging entrepreneur as courageous.

Obviously, making a decision requires courage — because it can be wrong as well as right.

But the entrepreneur has no choice: He has to be decisive, to be unafraid to make decisions.

There is no need to make hasty or poorly thought-through decisions, but there is a need to simply make them.

This question, therefore, has no multiple-choice answers.

Without hesitation, the entrepreneur *has* to be decisive!

# WOULD YOU CHARACTERIZE
# YOURSELF AS ORGANIZED?

The towering 50-story high-rise and the simple one-story ranch house have something in common: Neither could exist without a strong foundation.

Similarly, your new enterprise will be unable to exist if you do not have the organizational skills to anchor its objectives and operations.

So many things will be happening so fast that you will not be in a position to cope unless you are organized.

What does that mean in real life?

It means putting together a structure which will enable you to keep track of all categories of things — and to be able to find them and respond to them without any significant waste of time or energy.

It also means putting together a system which will enable your employees to look to a reliable source for direction, for information, for the ability to perform and perfect their tasks without disrupting the organization.

In straightforward language, it means *getting things together, keeping things together, being unafraid of details, details, details!*

Some entrepreneurs don't enjoy dealing with details, preferring to deal with the "big idea" or the "big picture."

If you might be one of them, simply keep this in mind: Without being organized and attending to the details, there soon may not be any picture at all!

QUESTION

# 55

## WOULD YOU CHARACTERIZE
## YOURSELF AS A
## "DAY-DREAMER?"

"Yes!" is a wonderful answer to this question — because day-dreaming is a wonderful quality for an entrepreneur.

We're not suggesting that you should fall asleep at the wheel while driving on the interstate — but we are noting that day dreams often lead to new inspirations and new ideas — and isn't that much of what being an entrepreneur is all about?

So if you find yourself frequently fantasizing or thinking up odd schemes, terrific!

Obviously, you shouldn't overdo it or mistake daydreams for reality, but as the launching pad for surprisingly inventive thoughts or unexpected solutions to sticky problems, day-dreaming is an entirely appropriate characteristic for an emerging entrepreneur!

# 56

## WOULD YOU CHARACTERIZE YOURSELF AS A SELF-STARTER?

For several years, there's been a device on the market for automobile owners who live in colder parts of the country: A remote-controlled starter which enables you to start your car by pushing a button while you're still inside the warmth and comfort of your house. By the time you're ready to leave, your car is warm and ready to go.

There is no similar device on the market for entrepreneurs — *and there isn't a self-respecting entrepreneur alive who would even think of using such a device if it were available!*

SELF-STARTING IS WHAT BEING AN ENTREPRENEUR IS ALL ABOUT IT!

IT'S AS ESSENTIAL TO THE ENTREPRENEUR AS AIR!

NO ENTREPRENEUR CAN LIVE WITHOUT IT!

So you can ignore this question.

Not because it's unimportant — but because, if you've come this far, you know that the typical entrepreneur's favorite two-letter word is . . . GO!

# 57

# HOW WOULD YOU
# DEFINE "INDEPENDENCE?"

Do you think of the anxious teen-ager's definition: Eager to be out on his own. Or the political scientist's definition: Self-governing. Or the economic definition: Acquiring enough money to be self-sufficient.

The healthy entrepreneur's definition has some of each of these qualities . . . plus one more: Humility.

The entrepreneur knows that being independent doesn't mean being free of dependence on others; the United States, for example, prides itself on its hard-won independence . . . but for how long would the USA remain independent if each of us didn't depend on one another . . . to stay independent?

Similarly, the entrepreneur knows that his independence depends on the good will of others.

The entrepreneur who forgets this rule will soon find himself losing his independence.

QUESTION

# 58

## HOW WOULD YOU DEFINE "PERSONAL FREEDOM?"

"Personal freedom" is a common catalyst and common objective for entrepreneurs-to-be.

The successful ones often achieve it — only to discover that it brings with it as much responsibility as freedom.

In its least complicated terms, personal freedom means the ability to go where you want to go when you want to go there — or to buy what you want to buy when you want to buy it.

Should you achieve this dimension of freedom, you will soon be as bored as you were when you didn't have it!

Just as money by itself is a poor reason for becoming an entrepreneur, this one-dimensional definition for personal freedom can often prove disappointing.

To the entrepreneur, personal freedom, like most aspects of being an independent businessperson, is a positive and productive objective.

It means being able to provide for yourself, your family, your community.

It is a definition which money can help to create — but which no amount of money can buy.

QUESTION

# 59

# HOW WOULD YOU
# DEFINE "ENTREPRENEUR?"

*The American Heritage Dictionary* says: An entrepreneur is "one who organizes, operates and especially assumes the risk of a business venture."

What is especially striking about this dictionary definition is that in a reference book which avoids bringing emotional meanings to words, it features the concept of "risk" with noticeable emphasis.

What would you emphasize in your definition?
*Freedom? Power? Security?*

We would emphasize HAPPINESS and PRODUCTIVITY — qualities which you wouldn't find in any dictionary.

To us, HAPPINESS and PRODUCTIVITY are what an entrepreneur is all about.

If an entrepreneur can create a sense of well-being and happiness for himself, his family and his community, he has accomplished something very significant.

If, in addition, he is productive and encourages a sense of productivity around him, he has accomplished something equally significant.

Thus, to us, an entrepreneur is someone who seeks HAPPINESS and PRODUCTIVITY.

The successful one achieves it.

The unsuccessful one has no regrets that he tried — and may well, in time, try again!

*What's your definition?*

QUESTION

# 60

## DO YOU LOOK FOR
## "SHORTCUTS"
## WHILE DOING BUSINESS?

There was a famous incident several years ago when a runner "won" a marathon — not by running all 26-plus miles but by entering at a late point in the race. Eventually, the ruse was uncovered — and the "victory" properly disqualified.

Are you a legitimate long-distance runner, or do you look for shortcuts wherever possible?

There's nothing wrong, of course, with being efficient — of doing a good job in the least amount of time — so long as the job isn't compromised.

But cutting corners — for the purpose of "getting away with something" — is a practice which will disqualify the entrepreneur in the marketplace as surely as our bogus winner was disqualified on the racecourse.

The entrepreneur has to give full value to his customers.

And the entrepreneur who is willing to compromise in that regard is one who will not be in business for long.

If cutting corners was something you occasionally did as an employee, take note that it is something that will quickly ruin you as an entrepreneur.

QUESTION

# 61

## DO YOU HAVE A GOOD REPUTATION IN YOUR BUSINESS COMMUNITY?

If this were not a business book, the question would probably read: Do you have a good reputation in your community?

The truth is that the entrepreneur will need to have a good reputation in both.

The business community — bankers, landlords, suppliers, etc. — will want to be reassured that you are an honest, reliable operator.

The community at large — your customers, your employees, your neighbors, etc. — will want to be reassured that you are a respectful and responsible citizen.

If, for one reason or another, your reputation has some blemishes (from a youthful indiscretion or whatever), your first order of business will be to repair the damage.

If your reputation is as strong as your determination to succeed as an entrepreneur, then you have a formidable asset going for you.

A good reputation evokes good feelings — and, more than most people, an entrepreneur is often judged by just such feelings.

QUESTION

# 62

# DOES YOUR FAMILY SUPPORT YOUR DECISION TO GO INTO BUSINESS FOR YOURSELF?

We've frequently spoken of the entrepreneur's courage throughout this book. We haven't yet directed our attention to the courage of the entrepreneur's family. It is equally essential and equally inspirational.

The entrepreneur requires the ability to draw on his own inner strength and resources — and on the strength of his family.

Without the love and support and commitment of his family, the entrepreneur will find himself on a long, lonely — and probably insurmountable — road!

Almost always a family will need some reassurance and patient explanation about the new path which the entrepreneur has chosen; the entrepreneur must provide that reassurance and patience without hesitation.

Starting a new business will always mean severe adjustments for the family — whether economic, social or even geographic.

The entrepreneur is prepared to deal with them; his family may not be.

Thus, the entrepreneur-to-be has to be especially sensitive and thoughtful about completely and honestly bringing his family into the process of beginning a business.

He must share his hopes — and his fears.

He must share the good news — and the bad.

He must, in other words, provide them with a realistic expectation of the road ahead.

The entrepreneur needs his family on his side.

Without it, he may have to re-consider the whole idea of going into business for himself.

With it, he will have the understanding and the support which a new businessman needs.

And, more often than not, that understanding and support can mean the difference between failing and succeeding!

QUESTION

# 63

## ONCE YOU'RE IN BUSINESS FOR YOURSELF, WILL YOU BE ABLE TO SLEEP AT NIGHT?

We don't mean this question literally — although insomnia can be an indication of discomfort or dissatisfaction with your life.

We're talking about a sense of inner calm, inner peace — the feeling that going into business for yourself is the absolutely right decision . . . for you!

We spoke of doubts early on — and the importance of resolving them before making this major move.

This is as good a time as any to remind you about that warning: If you're feeling uneasy about the possibility of being your own boss, of starting a new business (complete with all the risks), it's obviously still not too late to defer that decision until a time when contemplating the adventure of going into business for yourself brings you a more comfortable feeling.

Now we'll get back to the original question.

Most entrepreneurs report that, while they've never been busier, they also never slept better!

We suspect that it's the sleep of those who know that they're doing the right thing — and try to do it a little better every day!

QUESTION

# 64

# HOW DO YOU FEEL ABOUT
# THESE 64 QUESTIONS?

Our hope is that, at this point, you're feeling good about yourself — and good about the idea of going into business for yourself!

With any luck, these questions have helped you to focus on your weaknesses and strengths, your pluses and minuses, your certainties — and your doubts.

With a little more luck, they've confirmed what you've been feeling all along — that you are a strong candidate to become an entrepreneur.

There is no rush to making that move.

You may be eager to go into business now — or you may be thinking about it a couple of years away.

It really doesn't matter.

What does matter is that you feel confident and comfortable about that prospect.

If you do, then this book has succeeded — AND SO WILL YOU!

# THE SELF-EMPLOYMENT TEST CHECKLIST

The 64 questions on this Checklist are matched with the 64 chapters in this book. Each question asks for a YES or NO answer.

There are no absolute "right" or "wrong" answers to *The Self-Employment Test (SET)*, but most entrepreneurs *do* share certain common characteristics. Based on this knowledge, we developed *The SET Scale* to help you determine your personal self-employment potential.

Each page of the "test" is self-contained. The answers to the questions on each page are printed at the bottom of the page for easy, instant reference.

How do you shape up as an entrepreneur-in-the-making?

After taking the "test," we'll help you to interpret the meaning of your *SET Score*.

Good luck!

# THE 64 QUESTIONS

1 Are your reasons for going into
  business positive?                 Yes ☐   No ☐

2 Do you like who you see in the mirror?   Yes ☐   No ☐

3 Are you going into business out of anger?   Yes ☐   No ☐

4 Are you afraid of failing?   Yes ☐   No ☐

5 Are you afraid of succeeding?   Yes ☐   No ☐

6 Are you stubborn?   Yes ☐   No ☐

7 Are you persistent?   Yes ☐   No ☐

8 Are you confident?   Yes ☐   No ☐

9 Are you a leader?   Yes ☐   No ☐

10 Can you control yourself?   Yes ☐   No ☐

11 Can you control others?   Yes ☐   No ☐

12 Could you hire someone?   Yes ☐   No ☐

13 Could you fire someone?   Yes ☐   No ☐

14 Can you work with yourself?   Yes ☐   No ☐

15 Can you work with others?   Yes ☐   No ☐

16 Are you curious?   Yes ☐   No ☐

17 Are you creative?   Yes ☐   No ☐

18 Are you passionate?   Yes ☐   No ☐

19 Are you emotional?   Yes ☐   No ☐

20 Are you rational?   Yes ☐   No ☐

21 Can you be objective?   Yes ☐   No ☐

22 Are you afraid of taking risks?   Yes ☐   No ☐

23 Would you consider yourself a gambler?   Yes ☐   No ☐

---

### ANSWERS TO THE QUESTIONS ON THIS PAGE

| | | | |
|---|---|---|---|
| 1 Yes | 7 Yes | 13 Yes | 19 No |
| 2 Yes | 8 Yes | 14 Yes | 20 Yes |
| 3 No | 9 Yes | 15 Yes | 21 Yes |
| 4 No | 10 Yes | 16 Yes | 22 No |
| 5 No | 11 Yes | 17 Yes | 23 No |
| 6 Yes | 12 Yes | 18 Yes | |

24 Are you a single or oldest child?   Yes ☐   No ☐
25 Was your father an entrepreneur?   Yes ☐   No ☐
26 Did your mother work?   Yes ☐   No ☐
27 Were you lazy as a child?   Yes ☐   No ☐
28 Do you consider yourself "grown-up?"   Yes ☐   No ☐
29 Can you set goals?   Yes ☐   No ☐
30 Do you usually achieve your goals?   Yes ☐   No ☐
31 Do you have the ability to concentrate?   Yes ☐   No ☐
32 Are you in good health?   Yes ☐   No ☐
33 Do you have a high energy level?   Yes ☐   No ☐
34 Do you know how to "recharge" your batteries?   Yes ☐   No ☐
35 Do you trust yourself?   Yes ☐   No ☐
36 Do you trust others?   Yes ☐   No ☐
37 Do lawyers intimidate you?   Yes ☐   No ☐
38 Do accountants intimidate you?   Yes ☐   No ☐
39 Do bankers intimidate you?   Yes ☐   No ☐
40 Does the IRS intimidate you?   Yes ☐   No ☐
41 Are you ready to give up a regular paycheck?   Yes ☐   No ☐
42 Are you going into business only for the money?   Yes ☐   No ☐
43 Could you live without any money at all?   Yes ☐   No ☐
44 Can you write clearly?   Yes ☐   No ☐
45 Are you afraid of speaking in public?   Yes ☐   No ☐
46 Do you have the ability to listen?   Yes ☐   No ☐

### ANSWERS TO THE QUESTIONS ON THIS PAGE

| | | | |
|---|---|---|---|
| 24 Yes | 30 Yes | 36 Yes | 42 No |
| 25 Yes | 31 Yes | 37 No | 43 Yes |
| 26 Yes | 32 Yes | 38 No | 44 Yes |
| 27 No | 33 Yes | 39 No | 45 No |
| 28 Both | 34 Yes | 40 No | 46 Yes |
| 29 Yes | 35 Yes | 41 Yes | |

**47** Do you enjoy selling?     Yes ☐   No ☐
**48** Can you motivate others?     Yes ☐   No ☐
**49** Can you bounce back from setbacks?     Yes ☐   No ☐
**50** Do you know when to accept a defeat?     Yes ☐   No ☐
**51** Do you know your weaknesses?     Yes ☐   No ☐
**52** Do you know your strengths?     Yes ☐   No ☐
**53** Are you decisive?     Yes ☐   No ☐
**54** Are you organized?     Yes ☐   No ☐
**55** Do you often "daydream?"     Yes ☐   No ☐
**56** Are you a self-starter?     Yes ☐   No ☐
**57** Do you think independence requires dependence?     Yes ☐   No ☐
**58** Do you think money can buy "freedom?"     Yes ☐   No ☐
**59** Do you want to be happy and productive?     Yes ☐   No ☐
**60** Do you often look for "shortcut" solutions?     Yes ☐   No ☐
**61** Do you have a good business reputation?     Yes ☐   No ☐
**62** Is your family behind you?     Yes ☐   No ☐
**63** Will self-employment give you insomnia?     Yes ☐   No ☐
**64** Do you feel comfortable about going out on your own?     Yes ☐   No ☐

### ANSWERS TO THE QUESTIONS ON THIS PAGE

| | | | |
|---|---|---|---|
| **47** Yes | **51** Yes | **56** Yes | **61** Yes |
| **48** Yes | **52** Yes | **57** Yes | **62** Yes |
| **49** Yes | **53** Yes | **58** No | **63** No |
| **50** Yes | **54** Yes | **59** Yes | **64** Yes |
| | **55** Yes | **60** No | |

# HOW TO INTERPRET YOUR "SET" SCORE

Your *SET Score* is the total of all those answers which indicate your *Entrepreneurial Characteristics*. That total determines your current *Entrepreneurial Potential:*

| *Number of Entrepreneurial Characteristics* | *Your Entrepreneurial Potential* |
|---|---|
| 64 - 55 | GO |
| 54 - 40 | GO SLOW |
| 39 - 0 | NO GO |

GO — You appear to be ready to make your move as an entrepreneur. Your self-employment instincts are very high, and therefore your chances for success as an independent businessperson are equally encouraging. Based on traditional entrepreneurial principles, your chances of success would seem to be above-average.

GO SLOW — Your self-employment instincts are encouraging. You may seriously contemplate the prospect of going into business for yourself but should do so at a cautious pace. Over time, your *SET Score* will most likely improve. Until then, we would advise caution without becoming discouraged: You *are* a promising future candidate for self-employment.

NO GO — At this time, you would probably be uncertain as a self-employed person — and, therefore, most likely unsuccessful. Your best bet is to put your entrepreneurial plans on "hold" until a time when your prospects for success are more encouraging.

# A CLOSING OBSERVATION

*The Self-Employment Test* is not a book designed to be read once and discarded or tucked into a dusty corner. It is designed to be used time and again.

Use it whenever you are thinking about going into business for yourself.

Use it when you are starting a new business.

Use it after you've been in business for a while.

Entrepreneurs, like successful athletes, never forget to practice the fundamentals — and entrepreneurial fundamentals are what *The Self-Employment Test* is all about.

# ABOUT THE AUTHOR

Steve Kahn is an attorney and entrepreneur. As an entrepreneur, he has created new businesses in publishing, cable television and real estate. He has been the Executive Producer of "The Miss American Teen-Ager Pageant" for the ABC Television Network and a feature columnist for The New York Times Syndicate with a weekly audience of ten million Sunday newspaper readers. As an attorney, he served as Special Counsel and Director of Investor Relations for the Tishman Real Estate & Construction Co., Inc. He holds a B.S. degree from New York University and a J.D. degree from New York Law School.

# ABOUT THE NO NONSENSE
# SUCCESS SERIES

More people than ever before are thinking about going into business for themselves — and the No Nonsense Success Guides have been created to provide useful information for this growing and ambitious audience. Look for these related No Nonsense Success Guides: *Getting Into The Mail Order Business... How To Run A Business Out Of Your Home... How To Own And Operate A Franchise... How (and Where) To Get The Money To Get Started... Getting Into The Consulting Business.*